Farmhouse interior at Tregaron, Cardiganshire; pencil drawing by J. Varley, 1812. The small number of contemporary interior pictures known frequently show a surprising quantity and variety of furniture. Included here we find a settle, cradle, armchair, long table, dresser, spinning wheel, two meal chests and five stools.

WELSH COUNTRY FURNITURE

Richard Bebb

Shire Publications Ltd

CONTENTS

An ancient tradition 3

The hearth and home 4

The craftsmen and their customers 11

Problems of dating 17

Development of styles 19

Regional types and preferences 25

Further reading 32

Places to visit 32

Published in 1997 by Shire Publications Ltd, Cromwell House, Church Street, Princes Risborough, Buckinghamshire HP27 9AA, UK. Copyright © 1994 by Richard Bebb. First edition 1994; reprinted 1997. Shire Album 301. ISBN 0 7478 0236 X.

All rights reserved. No part of this publication may be reproduced or transmitted in any form or by any means, electronic or mechanical, including photocopy, recording, or any information storage and retrieval system, without permission in writing from the publishers.

Printed in Great Britain by CIT Printing Services, Press Buildings, Merlins Bridge, Haverfordwest, Dyfed SA61 1XF.

British Library Cataloguing in Publication Data: Bebb, Richard. Welsh Country Furniture. – (Shire Album; No. 301). I. Title II. Series 749.22. ISBN 0-7478-0236-X.

ACKNOWLEDGEMENTS
I wish to thank Dr William Linnard for allowing me to use quotations from his translation of *An Autumn in Wales* (Cowbridge,1985) by Julius Rodenberg, who visited Llanfairfechan, Caernarfonshire, in 1856.

All photographs are reproduced by courtesy of Country Antiques (Wales), Kidwelly, Dyfed.

Cover: *A cricket table and spoon rack in oak and an armchair in elm, made in Carmarthenshire in the eighteenth century.*

NOTES
The Welsh language has its own words for many types of furniture, but there is considerable variation between areas. For the purposes of this book it was thought best to use only those terms in general usage.

The names of the old Welsh counties are used in this book to describe the areas of origin of types, designs and individual pieces of furniture.

Oak 'coffor bach', West Wales, 1750-80. Only 18 inches (46 cm) tall and 29 inches (74 cm) wide, this is a miniature version of the full-size chests found in the area. It is an exceptional example, decorated with an inlay of holly and bog-oak, the sections between the drawers opening to reveal secret compartments.

Part of an intricately carved oak roodscreen from the Conwy Valley, c.1525.

AN ANCIENT TRADITION

Wales is a mountainous country and until the late nineteenth century had a scattered population with few large towns. But it has its own history and culture and should not be viewed merely as a poor and remote region on the periphery of mainstream developments. Surviving illustrated texts from the twelfth century show how the ancient woodworking crafts were well established. The amount and type of timber available by right to individuals for house building is specified, and there are instructions, including drawings, on how plantations of trees are to be maintained by pruning. An ordinance of the thirteenth century gave specific rights to certain individuals to work in the Forest of Senghenydd, producing domestic articles for sale, including chests 'made from dead wood', bowls and dishes. Isolated churches still contain a wealth of carpentry from the fifteenth and sixteenth

centuries, the carved motifs often showing clear Celtic antecedents. Little is known about the craftsmen who produced this work, but their influence certainly spread across the border to many English churches.

Some of the earliest pieces of oak furniture, with the most authentic provenances of any in Britain and complete with armorial bearings and initials, come from sixteenth-century Welsh homes, including the great cupboard of John ap Maredudd (in the Burrell Collection) and the ceremonial chairs of Rhys ap Thomas (in the Welsh Folk Museum).

The tradition of craftsmanship in native timbers continued into the eighteenth and nineteenth centuries to produce the dressers, cupboards, chairs and tables which once filled the cottages and farmhouses of rural Wales.

3

Oak table, Cardiganshire, 1780-1820. A type found throughout Wales, in a variety of sizes and timbers, with the characteristic square chamfered legs, reversible top and deep end drawer.

THE HEARTH AND HOME

Although few furniture types are exclusive to Wales, the forms they take are often quite distinctive and relate to the way of life into which they fitted. Unfortunately for present-day usage, this can often mean narrow farmhouse tables with deep drawers which prevent comfortable use, chairs which are too low, round tables too large for occasional use and too small for dining, and forbidding cupboard beds.

The typical single-storey Welsh cottage of the eighteenth century comprised two rooms, a kitchen and a bedroom, possibly with a further sleeping area for children in the roofspace, reached by a ladder. In addition there may have been an attached dairy and byre. Most farmhouses, while having larger rooms, corresponded to the same basic pattern, although they would usually have been two-storey, and this

became the norm for rural and the new industrial dwellings as the nineteenth century progressed. When there were sufficient upstairs rooms, the ground-floor bedroom could become partially or wholly used as a parlour.

While surviving wills and inventories give us some indication of the type and quantity of furniture available at various social levels, we have to build up a picture from contemporary accounts and illustrations, together with present-day recollections, of how the pieces were actually placed.

The main room downstairs formed the kitchen and living area, and its focus was the large open hearth, later to be filled with a cast-iron range. A high-backed settle was placed opposite or at right angles to the fire, providing a draught-free sitting area where the family would gather

4

at night, and where guests could be entertained.

A German traveller who stayed at a farmhouse near Conwy in 1856 was captivated by the story-telling and singing, and left this description of the family room:

'The hearth with its shining black iron hobs was built into the wall, and a mighty wood fire was always kept burning under a well-scoured cauldron. Against the wall stood two massive dressers of brown polished wood, with fittings of shining brass; on one of them the jugs, glasses and china ornaments, on the other the blue cups, saucers and plates in much profusion.'

The chairs and stools in such a room would generally be low, and orientated towards the warmth, while tables would be small and portable enough to be moved if more space were required at the fireside. By far the most common form was the 'cricket' table, with a round top raised on three splayed legs (for stability on an uneven floor), often with an undertier. To judge by the quantity still available, every home had at least one, and they were still being made in the traditional form until the Second World War. Larger rectangular tables might be situated in the kitchen or dairy beneath a window. Often narrow in width and with deep drawers for utensils, they were primarily intended for food preparation. Many of them had loose reversible tops and different sides would have been used for working and eating. Only in the largest farmhouses was there room for a dining table with an attendant

Left: *Ash hoop-back stick chair, West Wales, 1760-1840. Low chairs were placed around the fireside, sometimes to be used with a spinning wheel. The top ends of the uprights in the back are split and wedged into the hoop, and dowels are used at every joint.*
Right: *Ash rocking chair with rope seat, Cardiganshire, 1760-1840. A rare type of joined chair, with the common Welsh feature of a cut-out design, found here on the stretchers.*

Teak settle, Pembrokeshire, 1840-80. This type was called 'setl' in the north and 'sgiw' in the south and was used as a draught screen or placed against a wall; the base may be open or fitted with a box or drawers. The high straight back and sledge feet are indicative of south-west Wales. Teak was used in the shipyards of Pembroke Dock.

Two typical designs of stool, which were used extensively around the home and not exclusively for milking.

Oak cricket table, North Wales, 1760-1820. Available in various sizes and with or without undertiers and stretchers. It is quite common to find a mixture of timbers, often with tops of sycamore or deal (which are easily scrubbed clean) on bases of oak or elm.

6

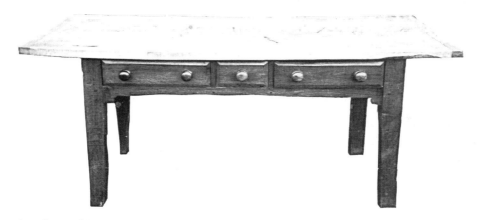

Oak dairy table with sycamore top, Meirionnydd, 1840-80. Sycamore was introduced from America by local mariners around 1730 and was valued for its resistance to the salty westerly winds and for the shelter it provided. Its close grain and lack of aroma made it ideal for dairy implements and it was frequently used for table tops.

Oak meal chest, Pembrokeshire, 1740-1800. Thomas Pennant visited a farm near Harlech in 1799 and found 'the furniture rude: the most remarkable are the "cistiau styffylog" or great oatmeal chests, which held the essential part of the provisions.'

Oak 'cwpwrdd deuddarn', Breconshire, 1720-60. Unlike the shorter English court cupboards, this type normally has drawers above the doors in the base and often exhibits highly individual features. Small drawers down the centre are not usual, although they can often be found behind a central door.

set of chairs, and this might be situated in the kitchen or the parlour. Tables with folding tops – round or rectangular – and with flaps which open from the side might also have been kept in either room and brought into the centre as required.

Some of the most easily recognisable Welsh pieces are the chests and cupboards made to store foodstuffs and utensils, and made to a far higher standard of construction and finish than their usage would suggest. Large meal chests, for example – found in peasant kitchens throughout Europe – were often finely panelled and polished, and pieces which we might assume were made for the parlour, such as the *cwpwrdd deuddarn* and *cwpwrdd tridarn* (two-part and three-part cupboards), were always meant for the kitchen. One of the dressers described by the German traveller was a *cwpwrdd tridarn* and still stands in the same home to this day, reputedly made from oak cut down on the farm itself.

Such cupboards could have held a variety of objects, but other types were more obviously intended to store food. Known as 'bread and cheese' cupboards, they have ventilated front panels formed by turned spindles or fretwork. The smaller ones, which might hang on a wall or, because of their weight, rest on a ledge, are akin to earlier types found throughout Britain. But others, normally two-piece, are peculiar to particular areas, and were especially common in Anglesey and Caernarfonshire.

Dressers are the pieces most commonly associated with Welsh homes and these form a continuum from extremely utilitarian types, little more than shelves over work tables, to purely decorative examples intended solely for display. Most examples perform both functions and fall somewhere in between, and it is difficult to ascertain the rules which governed their original position. Undoubtedly they were normally intended for the main living area, the kitchen, although those homes which had a separate parlour of sufficient importance may have had an additional one in that room.

While dressers are not exclusive to Wales, they do possess an attribute common to much Welsh furniture, that of making the best use of limited floor space. Whether made in one or two parts, most coffers, chests of drawers, press cupboards, corner cupboards, etc, are as tall as practical use would allow. This necessity was also catered for by the dual function of many pieces, especially favoured if they incorporated a seat. Many settles,

Oak food cupboard, Caernarfonshire, 1800-30. Often known as a 'bread and cheese' ('bara caws') cupboard, this type is generally associated with Anglesey and Llyn but can be found further south. The sides are of grained deal, which was frequently used in those areas where native timber was scarce.

particularly in the smaller homes of south-west Wales, had backs which swung forward to form a table. This can appear to be the most impracticable piece imaginable to us today, and very difficult to place, but its prevalence shows its former utility. Others known as 'bacon settles' had large cupboards built into their backs, although these would not necessarily have been used for hanging bacon.

The most often mentioned piece of furniture in early accounts is the bed, although few examples have survived. It was usually completely enclosed in a cupboard and might have been sited near the hearth (possibly with a seat attached to the front), or, more often, in the adjoining downstairs bedroom. In many one-roomed cottages the ends of two such beds formed the dividing wall and may even have had shelves attached to the outside. Besides low truckle beds, which could be pushed away under higher ones, additional beds might fold up into small cupboards. Especially when the downstairs bedroom was also used as a parlour, these could be quite elaborately disguised to resemble smart chests of drawers or cabinets.

Not all homes were equally well furnished, and the reports of government officials concerned with health, education and morality, and travellers' accounts, make harrowing and depressing reading. One description of North Wales records:

'One smoking hearth, for it should not be styled a kitchen, and a damp litter-cell, for it cannot be called a bedroom, are frequently all the space allotted to a labourer, his wife, and four or five children. The consequences are obvious; filth, disease and, frequently, premature death.'

But the enthusiastic German visitor, speaking of the same area, 'had to rejoice in the great cleanliness which prevailed even in the poorest hovels. Everywhere the stone floor, the bright windows, the kitchen and the dresser with its blue china.'

9

Oak dresser, Denbighshire, 1700-20. High-quality workmanship, including in this case cushion-moulded drawers, is often encountered in pieces clearly intended for small homes, this example being only 73 inches (185 cm) high and 50 inches (127 cm) wide.

Oak chest of drawers, Carmarthenshire, 1780-1830. With a height of 51 inches (130 cm), this is not particularly tall for what are known locally as 'half-chests' or 'half-drawers'. The inlaid frieze, canted corners and pretty bracket feet are all features found on the related coffers, chests on chests and linen presses.

Oak post bed, Montgomeryshire, eighteenth century. The timber is roughly shaped with an adze and painted red. Sacking originally hung from the posts, and there was a mattress of straw.

The underside of the table shown on the front cover. This is not the most usual form, which would be constructed with mortise and tenon joints. The ends of each piece fit into round holes in the others and into the top. It has a very sophisticated appearance and is the work of a turner, who would have produced a variety of objects for the home and farm.

THE CRAFTSMEN AND THEIR CUSTOMERS

Most surviving furniture dates from the last three centuries, leading to the widespread impression that very little existed previously, especially in poorer homes. This is, however, more likely to be due to the low rate of survival, and most houses may have been more comfortably furnished than we have thought. We know that the skills required for the manipulation of timber were developed from a very early period for house building and the production of carts and agricultural implements, and furniture making would have used the methods and styles appropriate to those related crafts.

In many rural communities such techniques continued into the twentieth century, and we find a considerable overlap in the overall appearance of furniture and practical items such as spinning wheels and cheese presses.

One of the earliest and most versatile forms of construction is the stick variety, where split and simply shaped pieces are inserted into a central plank. Using green timber, held with dowels or wedges, this method was used on stools, chairs, benches and tables. Crude as the method may seem, great skill was required to produce serviceable everyday furniture, which was invariably made of well-figured timber, usually ash or elm. The technique permits enormous variety, and many examples are quite sophisticated and were not always merely a cheap alternative.

A second category of furniture, primarily chairs and cradles, was that made from lipwork – coiled basketry formed of ropes of straw – which was also used to produce beehives, corn measures, chimneys and coffins. Wheat straw was an important fodder crop and was widely available for many purposes. To form the basketwork, a handful of straw is pushed through the fist and the emerging rope is bound with holly, bramble or peeled and split lengths of willow. The shape of the article is built up directly as the rope is produced, each succeeding layer being bound to the previous one. It can be assumed that surviving examples represent a minute proportion of the original number, because of the susceptibility of the material to

11

numerous in Wales than elsewhere, and the quality of the panelling in particular is exceptional. Some of this work was performed in workshops on the large estates and in the small market towns, increasingly so during the nineteenth century. There skilled joiners used local, commercially grown ash and oak, and imported deal, which was initially used only as a secondary timber for backboards and internal parts. In the more exposed western coastal areas, where trees were scarce, more furniture was made entirely from deal, which was usually painted, often, but not invariably, in imitation of more expensive woods.

But most furniture was produced in the countryside, where there is less evidence of an organised craft, with hardly any mentions in trade directories or references to apprentices. It is probable that only a small

Oak cheese press, Carmarthenshire, 1800-40. A great deal of care has gone into this design, which gives the appearance of a piece of household furniture. It uses several methods of construction, and the style of the base, which is the simplest form of bench, recurs in spinning wheels, settles and chairs.

damp, woodworm and vermin. It is nevertheless surprising that virtually every piece known has been designed and built up in a different way, reflecting the adaptability of the method and the inventiveness of the makers, who were specialists in this craft.

The bulk of Welsh furniture was produced using the techniques of joinery, whereby squared sections of seasoned timber are fixed together by mortise and tenon joints and held by dowels. The types and designs produced in this way are more

Ash and elm stick chair, 1760-1840. Difficult to date and probably impossible to ascribe to a particular area. Chairs of this kind are normally quite plain, often with three legs, but can have shaped combs, turned uprights, and occasionally shaped back splats.

12

of their customers, often showing great ingenuity. The timber they used was locally grown, and there was a marked preference for oak grown on the farm itself. Such furniture is characterised by having dense well-figured timber even in the backboards and drawer linings. A diarist recalling his childhood in Carmarthenshire in the early nineteenth century remembered that:

'Itinerant furniture makers used to go round the farmhouses, where they were given board and lodging, to work up the timber, cut and seasoned on the farm, into furniture, beds, tables, chairs, kitchen dressers etc. Especially noteworthy were the excellent roomy bureaux which were strongly made, with well proportioned mouldings and fretwork of conventional pattern, and a simple inlay of native woods such as box and yew.'

Many pieces show a combination of methods of construction, something we would not expect in the work of a time-served joiner. The fronts of finely panelled coffers, for example, are often nailed to plain boarded sides, and panelled chairs might have simple stick legs. Some of the most competent joined furniture comes from Snowdonia, where dovetails, which are specific to furniture making, were apparently never used. The craftsmen had a range of skills and used whichever seemed appropriate at the time.

The practice of local carpenters providing goods to the particular requirements of their neighbours extended into the beginning of the twentieth century. Daybooks kept by John Thomas and William Parry of Llanbedr in Meirionnydd from 1882 to 1900 give details of an enormous variety of woodwork, from shop fitments and chapel pews to waterwheels and axe handles, and including corn chests, round

number of rural craftsmen of any sort were able to make a living without other income, and many would have considered themselves primarily farmers. Robert Williams, who appears in Vosper's evocative painting of 'Salem', was a 'carpenter and farmer', sharing his exposed hill farm with two brothers. Others, often combining carpentry with masonry, occupied small farms and travelled around their locality as the seasons permitted. The isolation of many rural areas limited the market for their skills but also protected them from competition, leading to the development of highly individual local styles. The furniture they made was based on traditional forms and evolved with the needs

13

Oak hanging press, Caernarfonshire, 1730-60. This style of panelling is found on dressers and cupboards in Snowdonia. Made throughout of the dense oak typical of exposed windswept upland areas, where the timber grows very slowly in shallow soils.

The backs of many cupboards and chests are as carefully constructed as the fronts. Equally often, however, especially in West Wales, panelled fronts are simply nailed to boarded sides and backs. These would possibly be the work of two men working together, and the timber itself is always identical.

tables, chests of drawers, settles, cradles, children's chairs and glazed cupboards. They made something different every day, using a variety of techniques, often working on site and using timber cut and sawn on their customers' farms. A century later, examples of their work remain, providing service in their original locations.

14

The tiny workshop of the carpenter Robert Williams, who appears in the famous 'Salem' painting. From this remote location above Harlech, Meirionnydd, he produced both furniture and implements for his neighbours.

The top of the table on page 7, showing the joint between the two top boards and the pattern formed by the oak dowels. This was a favourite method in Wales, and often used on coffer lids and cupboard sides.

Painted deal washstand, Pembrokeshire, 1870-1900. This decoration does not attempt to imitate other timbers but uses the technique of graining to produce a traditional pattern which was also found on the beaten earth floors of the county.

15

Oak settle with a folding back which converts to a table, Cardiganshire,1730-60. The rear leaf is fixed in the horizontal position, while the back of the settle lifts and rests on brackets. It was found in a chapel in Rhydlewis and was probably used as a pulpit/communion table in the period when dissenters and nonconformists met in farmhouses.

The underside of the chair shown on the cover. The maker clearly produced a variety of articles, using whichever method seemed appropriate. The square front legs are fixed with mortise and tenon joints, but the single rear leg is wedged through the seat (which is shaped like the milking stool shown on page 6). The back uprights pass down through the seat and are held with large dowels passing through at right angles.

Oak cradle, Breconshire,1740-80. The single boards forming the sides are nailed to the ends with the upright posts acting as strengtheners. This method is found on utilitarian chests from the earliest times into the twentieth century.

PROBLEMS OF DATING

Precise dating of traditional furniture can be a frustrating task, as people's requirements and craft methods remained unchanged for generations. Items in everyday use may also show undue signs of wear and a rapid build-up of surface patination. The combinations of techniques employed by some carpenters and their preference for local woods also cause problems, and primitive construction and dark heavy timber are not necessarily signs of great age. Many pieces appear very early in their basic form, but very late in some of their details. However, the common view that because much Welsh furniture is demonstrably late it must all be is equally false and most styles were made over a very long period.

Nevertheless, some forms are associated with more definite periods than others, and the relatively small number of pieces known which bear authentic initials and dates, or with inscribed makers' marks or family documentation, enable us to pinpoint styles and chart developments.

This information is helpful mainly in the analysis of particular furniture types in fairly restricted areas and it is difficult to generalise. For example, there was a gradual change in the design of cupboard doors from those with flat recessed panels, to raised and fielded panels, through to flat panels within shaped frames, and finally to shaped panels applied over the frame. But this sequence took place at different rates in different areas and there was much overlapping, many observed differences being ones of quality and individual workmanship rather than age.

Oak clock case, Montgomeryshire, dated 1769. When fitted with original movements, clock cases can be precisely dated and give clues to dating other pieces from their area. The clock itself is by Samuel Roberts of Llanfair Caereinion, who finished the work on 21st December 1768 for Evan Hugh, at a cost of £2 5s 0d.

Oak linen press, Carmarthenshire, 1800-30. Linen presses were produced in a number of sizes and designs and with a variety of optional embellishments, such as the side columns and false drawer in the top section of this example. The internal parts and backboards are of deal. Great differences are encountered, and it is not always clear if they are due to quality or period.

18

Left: *Glazed oak corner cupboard, Carmarthenshire, 1790-1820. Freestanding two-part corner cupboards had either solid or glass doors in the top section, although the latter is much less common outside the south-west.*
Right: *Oak bureau bookcase, Carmarthenshire, 1780-1820. These are frequently of squat proportions, since the height of the base is determined by its use as a desk, and any accommodation to a low ceiling has to be made in the top half.*

DEVELOPMENT OF STYLES

Welsh furniture is thought of as essentially plain and functional but is characterised by restrained decorative features, and the surface is always well finished and full of colour. Each piece was an important acquisition, intended to be handed down, and there was an expectation that it would have an individual character. Many commentators have described the importance of the 'hearth and home' and the associations which accumulated around the highly polished furniture and gleaming china.

It is important to remember the size of house and the social class we are considering when comparing furniture, but in rural Wales distinctions were not great in this period. In each area most dwellings had the same basic layout and the same combination of furniture, although the quality might vary. Apart from the small number of gentry, who had different motivations and were catered for by different craftsmen, and the very poor, most farmers and their labourers, the clergy and even minor gentry were part of the same local society and fulfilled their expectations within its traditions.

Throughout the eighteenth and nineteenth centuries there was a growing emphasis on comfort and display, and styles became more distinctive. Although the family room always remained the kitchen, increasing importance attached to the parlour. Even in the one-up one-down houses of the new industrial towns, one part of

Oak clock case, Llandeilo, Carmarthenshire, 1820-30. Although it contains a simple thirty-hour movement with a painted enamel dial, nothing was spared on the production of the nicely proportioned and decorated case, which is constructed of the most heavily figured oak, including the one-piece backboard.

the downstairs room became the 'best' half. In this room would be found pieces suitable for displaying ornaments or books, usually cupboards or chests with a glazed upper section and sometimes fitted into a corner, possibly an additional dresser, and perhaps a longcase clock and a bureau.

The ownership of a longcase clock was an important ambition, and clockmakers flourished in most communities. Many of the movements themselves were quite basic, because of ease of maintenance in isolated farmhouses as much as cost. It is often the cases which appear more important, exhibiting all of the care and ingenuity found in the best work of the carpenter. There was no universally preferred position, but the clock was always given prominence and in many areas, especially in the north, stood alongside the dresser – often on a slate plinth.

Bureaux, sometimes with a cupboard on top, and generally of large and squat proportions, spread rapidly from the mid eighteenth century, when Wales was one of the most literate countries in Europe. Nonconformity claimed the overwhelming allegiance of the population and great emphasis was placed on the ability of its adherents to read the Bible and Catechism for themselves. Education was promoted through circulating schools and Sunday schools, both of which might be held in farmhouses. These desks were frequently inlaid with the owners' initials, and from these we know that they were often made for relatively lowly homes and were sometimes owned by women.

There was a similar increase in the variety of pieces available for the bedrooms, to accommodate the greater quantity of blankets and clothing. Coffers, cupboards and chests of drawers were produced in an infinite number of combinations with various degrees of elaboration and were especially numerous in the south-west. The tall coffers with fielded Gothic panels and drawers beneath are particularly distinctive and were offered with lift-up lids or opening fronts. The degree of attention paid to these pieces, which would perhaps not normally be seen by many people, implies their connection with a marriage. One of the most prized pieces was a miniature version, the *coffor bach*, which invariably has important associations for its owners, often because a family history suggests it was part of a dowry. Coffers and boxes of various sizes are the most likely types to be elaborated with an impressive form of inlaid decoration which was widespread in a number of areas, particularly south Pembrokeshire, north Carmarthenshire and the Vale of Glamorgan. In this tradition, a flowing pattern was cut into the surface of the frame and panels, into which were laid pieces of timber of contrasting colour, usually holly or sycamore and bog-oak. This may have been an optional extra, available at an additional cost, and

Oak coffer, Carmarthenshire, 1760-1800. Chests with drawers in the base were for holding clothing and blankets and can be very tall, 48 inches (122 cm) in this case. A distinguishing Welsh feature is the form of hinge, using two long wooden pieces under the lid which slot into the backboard.

Oak coffer, Pembrokeshire, 1750-90. Many similar examples of restrained inlay of flowing geometric and floral patterns have been recorded, all of them different and showing a variety of derivations. They were not the work of specialist inlayers, but of the same craftsmen who made the furniture.

Oak cupboard on chest, Meirionnydd, 1740-60. This is unique, although each element can be found on other pieces. The raised and fielded Gothic-panelled doors enclose a cupboard with shaped shelves. The elaborate pediment has a fretted comma design, and the frieze has a blind-fretted pattern of a type which is frequently inlaid. The internal parts are of sycamore.

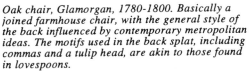

Oak chair, Glamorgan, 1780-1800. Basically a joined farmhouse chair, with the general style of the back influenced by contemporary metropolitan ideas. The motifs used in the back splat, including commas and a tulip head, are akin to those found in lovespoons.

Oak potboard dresser, Montgomeryshire,1740-70. Dressers from this area are of the highest workmanship and made of the reddish black oak found in the moorland regions. Although of the same basic proportions, they show great variety in their details, and this example has heart-shaped fretwork below the cornice.

was certainly reserved for pieces of special significance. More basic designs, including initials and dates, were found over a wider area of Wales, but normally still on special pieces such as longcase clocks and bureaux.

Welsh furniture showed a great capacity for development because of the positive preference shown by even relatively well-off members of the community for traditional furniture made by local craftsmen, but incorporating extra flourishes and details. They may have required this to underline their status but more often perhaps to mark important occasions. Convention did not govern precisely how a piece should look. A variety of alternatives was possible, and an innovative craftsman could be relied upon to produce something special. It had always been part of this dynamic tradition that no two pieces were identical, and inspiration was drawn from a number of sources, and even designs from fashionable urban furniture could be accommodated when deemed appropriate.

The process can be seen in dressers, which were virtually a symbol for the home and frequently descended through the female line. They exhibit enormous variety even within small localities, and pieces clearly from the same workshop will each contain unique combinations of fretwork, turnings and drawer arrangements. There was no precise correlation with wealth, but the most prosperous farmhouses in each area wanted the finest dressers, from the Vale of Glamorgan through Montgomeryshire to the Vale of Clwyd.

The particular sentiments attached to the dresser ensured its continuous production and development, even in the industrialised areas of south-east Wales, which retained their cultural links with the countryside. As the quantity of valued ornaments increased, the open racks acquired glazed sections, and the 'dog-kennel' in the base, formerly used for a stoneware crock of eggs or butter, now held a sewing machine. Changing requirements had always produced new forms in the Welsh tradition, and such dressers remained fashionable in the Valleys well into the twentieth century.

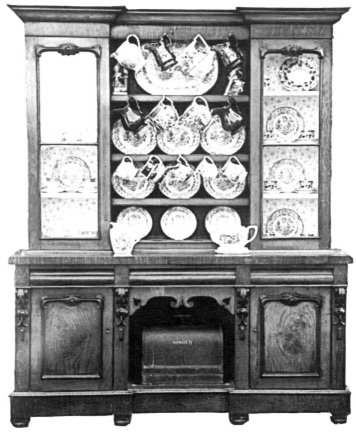

Glazed oak dresser, Carmarthenshire. This is a development of the West Wales 'dog-kennel' dresser, known locally as a 'seld', by the addition of glazed cupboards. This piece has a number of walnut and mahogany embellishments which are found on various styles of cupboard from about 1870. It was made in 1912 by David Davies of Llandeilo, a furniture maker and wheelwright, for the wedding of his nephew.

Left: *Oak armchair, Carmarthenshire, 1700-30. The broad proportions and bold use of timber suggest that this is a Welsh chair, but without a provenance we could not easily guess from which area.*
Right: *Children's oak chairs, Pembrokeshire, 1820-60. Scaled-down versions of a basic chair type found throughout Wales with an enormous variation in the back designs. It is proving difficult to assign designs to particular areas, although some may be the products of specialist chairmakers, such as John Davies and John Jones, who worked in Pontardulais, Glamorgan, in the 1820s.*

REGIONAL TYPES AND PREFERENCES

Some of the variations we find are associated with definite localities, although a comprehensive description of Welsh furniture on that basis remains elusive. In terms of material culture, Wales itself is not a discrete region, and certain parts have more in common with neighbouring areas of the British Isles than with the rest of the Principality. It might be more enlightening to talk of the Welsh Borders area or the Bristol Channel area than to talk of typical furniture from Montgomeryshire or Glamorgan. If Wales were to be divided into regions it is difficult to know whether it should be on the basis of counties (old or new), valleys, simply north and south, or perhaps the central moorlands and the coast. Different categories would seem appropriate in different cases.

Unfortunately, much furniture has already long been dispersed from its original location, as individuals moved or inherited from distant relatives. During the nineteenth century in particular there were large-scale migrations to the new industrial valleys. The present location of longcase clocks, which reveal the maker's town or village, indicates how far people moved, often in unexpected directions, and shows that they took their valued possessions with them. Carpenters also moved, transferring their methods and ideas to new areas. In the remoter valleys styles may have been determined by the overlapping movements of various semi-itinerant carpenters, whose work is therefore not found in easily demarcated areas.

Problems arise when a piece is said to originate in a particular place and then all

*Oak 'cwpwrdd gwydr' (glazed cupboard),
Caernarfonshire, 1850-80. These were found in
many parlours and their details mirror the open-
top dressers of the area, especially in the use of
grained deal for the sides and large pieces of
exotic timbers for decorative inlay. They
originally held rows of theological books as well
as tea services and souvenirs, but in the
twentieth century the latter became more usual.*

*Oak 'cwpwrdd tridarn', Conwy Valley, Caernarfonshire, dated 1731. These were the most
treasured pieces in the North Wales farmhouses for which they were made, often by tradition
of oak grown on the farm itself. This example has many superior features including original
carving and shaped splats both in a style associated with the valley, owners' initials and date,
secret locks, and a geometric design inlaid with pieces of contrasting colour.*

vaguely similar pieces, regardless of
where they are found, are assigned to the
same area. This often obscures the widespread distribution of certain types, such
as stick chairs, and assumes that the ini-
tial attribution was correct.

Many individual pieces clearly form part
of recognisable groups on the basis of
style or constructional details. They are
normally described as being from a particular county, although they are often the
product of a single carpenter or workshop
and not necessarily representative of a
wider area. A large number of the oak
dressers and glazed cupboards from
Anglesey, for example, have the same
panelled deal sides and turned and inlaid
mahogany embellishments. It should be
possible to identify many such groups and
eventually assign them to relatively small
areas. Broader generalisations about regional types have in the past tended to be
wrong, or at the very least misleading.

Nevertheless there are observable differences between certain areas, particularly in the cases of dressers and panelled

chests and cupboards, and two examples illustrate this. The *cwpwrdd tridarn* is associated with the early history of the cupboard-base dresser and developed from the more widely available court cupboard through the addition of a top tier for display purposes. It was produced in an exciting variety in local oak for the larger farmhouses of north-west Wales from about 1680 to 1780, many examples being dated. It was clearly made by a number of different carpenters, who also produced related pieces, but it does not appear to have spread to a much wider area. Similarly, in south-west Wales the 'Carmarthen coffer', a wide low linen press, often of great quality and with the appearance of a tall coffer, was once common but does not appear further north. Differences such as these may be the result of the requirements of subtly different ways of life, and we should study such cupboards as components of larger combinations of furniture to see how various needs were fulfilled in different ways. In other cases we may be comparing pieces from different periods rather than different areas, and certainly much of the furniture from North Wales appears older than that normally found in the more highly populated south. Whether this is true or not, there is no reason to suppose in such instances that the furniture from one area evolved from that of another. All parts of Wales contain early examples and share a long history of fine carpentry.

As in other European cultures, the dresser is the most prestigious piece and exhibits the most recognisable local variations. It was always thought that a simple division existed between certain main types of dresser, with cupboard bases in

Oak 'Carmarthen coffer', western Glamorgan, 1800-30. Many coffers with lift-up lids have been converted to this more useful type of cupboard, the telltale signs being the presence of a keyhole and hinge marks.

Oak cupboard-base dresser, Cardiganshire, 1790-1820. The base is identical to that found on the typical 'cwpwrdd deuddarn' from this area, in which potboard bases are thought more usual. This rack could be duplicated on both potboard and 'dog-kennel' dressers.

the north and open potboard bases in Mid Wales and the south. But it seems probable that both general types existed in most districts, sometimes offered as alternatives by the same carpenter, and such a distinction is not particularly useful in disentangling the incredible variety encountered. Many homes had two dressers, presenting a number of options for storage and display. While the cupboard bases held food and smaller utensils, the potboards originally held larger containers for the preparation and storage of dairy products, and this may account for the

greater preponderance in the south and west, where butter was produced for local and West Country markets from an early period.

From the late eighteenth century the display function of the dresser increased, and this became its sole purpose in the finer potboard examples which were kept in the parlour. There would be an additional, more utilitarian dresser, probably with cupboards, in the kitchen. Display was apparently a more important criterion in the increasingly prosperous south, the typical example being alive with brightly

28

coloured china bought at local fairs, with copper lustre jugs hanging from each shelf. In contrast, dressers from Mid and North Wales, even when they had potboards, were more sedately decorated, perhaps with a single service of blue and white plates, and are rarely found with hooks on the shelves.

The discovery of quite specific local types is more fruitful than the attempt to divide Wales into regions, and many attributions in the past have become self perpetuating myths. The main features of the 'Swansea Valley' dresser for example, with its shaped rack and spice drawers, are found over a wide part of South Wales, and it is itself not the only type found in that valley. Similarly, the distinctively squat and clearly early panelled-base dressers of Snowdonia emanate from a very sparsely populated area, which supported few carpenters, and are not representative of the whole of North Wales. Even in this remote district potboard dressers are known, although if taken from their surroundings they would

Oak potboard dresser, possibly north-west Wales, 1750-80. This represents a stage in the development from the utilitarian dairy dressers which held equipment for making butter and cheese. The height of the base in relation to the rack is the same as that found on cupboard-base dressers from the north.

Oak potboard dresser, Cardiganshire, 1820-50. Even the plainest dressers from this area were covered with an array of colourful pottery and keepsakes, bought by the farmers' wives with their 'egg money'. The potboard base held stoneware crocks and sycamore dairy implements. The backboards, shelves and potboard are of deal.

undoubtedly be classed as from South Wales.

The inevitable break-up of the rural economy did not take place at the same rate in all areas, but in Wales as elsewhere furniture gradually ceased to have particularly local characteristics. In 1896 Thomas E. Ellis MP lamented the end of an era and the central part furniture had played in it:

'What was the main feature of the furniture of an old Welsh farmhouse? Not a pretentious and characterless cupboard with a thin veneer over badly-seasoned and cracking timber and with loose and rickety hinges, but the *cwpwrdd tridarn* – a shapely and substantial cupboard of solid and seasoned oak. It is well proportioned, it is shapely; perhaps there is a dainty bit of carving on it, a few initials and perchance a date. At any rate, it is serviceable, it has served not one generation but three, five, eight generations in that hearth and home. Are you surprised that there should be in Wales that strong affection and attachment to hearth and home, which very much puzzle the modern man, but which I think are a glory and a strength to the Welsh character and the Welsh nation. I need only mention other features of the furniture and economy of a Welsh house, the dresser, the settle, the arm chair, the table, the eight-day clock, which unconsciously carry a message from generation to generation, and add to the wealth of associations and to the hereditary enjoyment of a home.'

30

*Oak cupboard-base dresser, Snow-
donia, 1730-60. Dressers from this
area are substantial and with their
overhanging racks and deep fielded
panelling have the appearance of a
cupboard. Made of a well-figured and
extremely dense oak, this would have
been made on the farm itself from
timber cut and sawn there. Unusually,
the central portion, which is normally
fixed, falls forward to reveal a narrow
cupboard.*

*Oak 'cwpwrdd tridarn',
Caernarfonshire, 1730-60. This example
stood in a large farmhouse kitchen
alongside a dresser and contained the
'jugs, glasses and china ornaments in
much profusion', which so impressed a
German visitor in 1856.*

FURTHER READING

Brown, John. *Welsh Stick Chairs*. Abercastle Publications, Fishguard, 1990. The views and experiences of a modern craftsman.

Chinnery, Victor. *Oak Furniture: The British Tradition*. Antique Collectors Club, Woodbridge, 1979.

Davies, T. Alun. *The Welsh Dresser*. University of Wales Press, Cardiff, 1991.

Gilbert, Christopher. *English Vernacular Furniture 1750-1900*. Yale University Press, London, 1991. A good exposition of the methodology of vernacular furniture studies.

Jenkins, David. *The Agricultural Community in South West Wales*. University of Wales Press, Cardiff, 1971.

Jenkins, J. Geraint. *Life and Tradition in Rural Wales*. Alan Sutton, Stroud, 1991.

Pryce, W. T. R., and Davies, T. Alun. *Samuel Roberts Clockmaker*. National Museum of Wales, Cardiff, 1985. An in-depth study of the life of an eighteenth-century rural craftsman.

Smith, Peter. *Houses of the Welsh Countryside*. HMSO, London, 1975.

Twiston-Davies, L., and Lloyd-Johnes, H. J. *Welsh Furniture*. University of Wales Press, Cardiff, 1950.

PLACES TO VISIT

Museum displays may be altered and intending visitors are advised to check that relevant items are on show and to find out opening times before travelling.

Museum of Welsh Life, St Fagans, Cardiff CF5 6XB. Telephone: 01222 569441. This is the National Collection, where a large variety of superb pieces is displayed in vernacular buildings re-erected from sites throughout Wales.

Smaller, but interesting, collections can be found at:

Aberconwy House, 2 Castle Street, Conwy, Gwynedd LL32 8AY. Telephone: 01492 592246.

Abergavenny Museum, The Castle, Castle Street, Abergavenny, Gwent NP7 5EE. Telephone: 01873 854282.

Bangor Museum and Art Gallery, Ffordd Gwynedd, Bangor, Gwynedd LL57 1DT. Telephone: 01248 353368.

Brecknock Museum, Captain's Walk, Brecon, Powys LD3 7DW. Telephone: 01874 624121.

Carmarthen Museum, Abergwili, Carmarthen, Dyfed SA31 2JG. Telephone: 01267 231691.

Ceredigion Museum, Coliseum, Terrace Road, Aberystwyth, Dyfed SY23 2AQ. Telephone: 01970 634212.

Erddig, near Wrexham, Clwyd LL13 0YT. Telephone: 01978 313333.

Swansea Museum, Victoria Road, Swansea, West Glamorgan SA1 1SN. Telephone: 01792 653763.

Tudor Merchant's House, Quay Hill, Tenby, Dyfed SA70 7BX. Telephone: 01834 842279.

Ty Mawr Wybrnant, near Penmachno, Gwynedd LL25 0HJ. Telephone: 01690 760213.